Together We Pray

PRAYERS TO KNOW BY HEART

CASTLE POINT BOOKS
NEW YORK

www.castlepointbooks.com

The Castle Point Books trademark is owned by Castle Point Publishing, LLC.
Castle Point books are published and distributed by St. Martin's Publishing Group.

ISBN 978-1-250-27760-2 (paper-over-board)

Design by Joanna Williams
Images used under license from Shutterstock.com

Our books may be purchased in bulk for promotional, educational, or business use.
Please contact your local bookseller or the Macmillan Corporate and Premium Sales Department
at 1-800-221-7945, extension 5442, or by email at MacmillanSpecialMarkets@macmillan.com.

First Edition: 2021

10 9 8 7 6 5 4 3 2 1

THIS BOOK BELONGS TO:

....

Contents

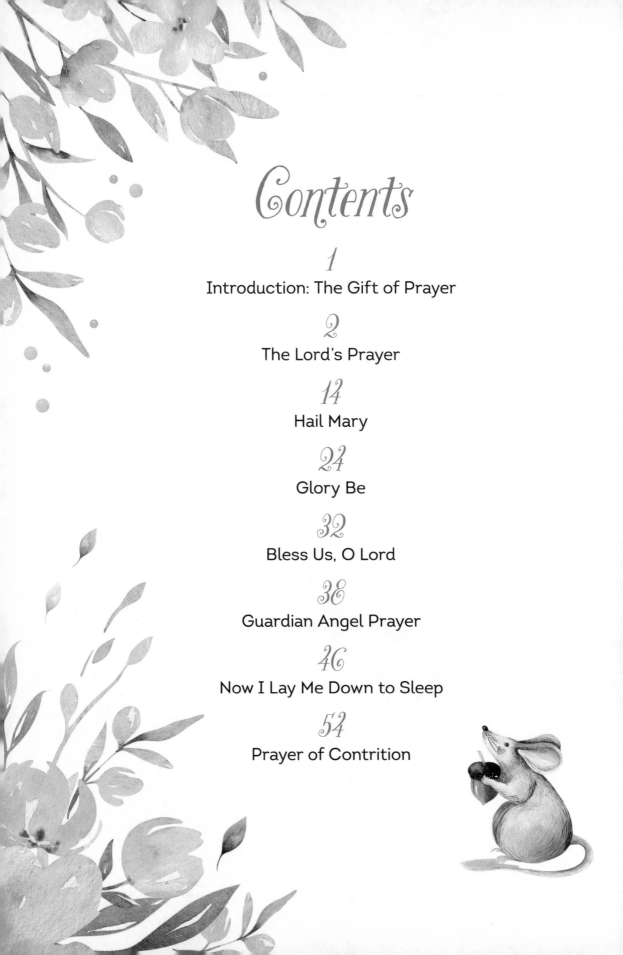

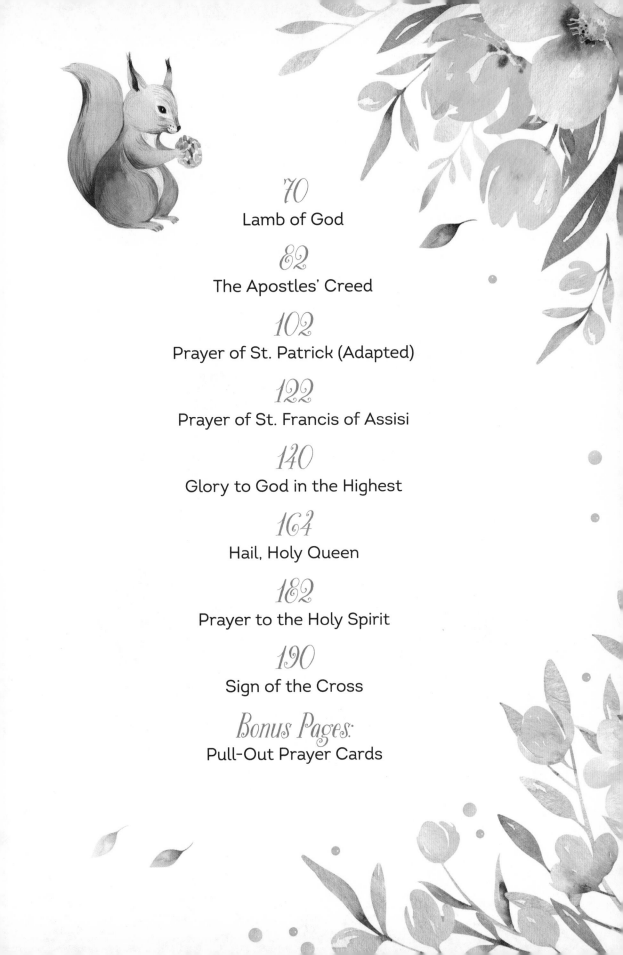

Introduction
The Gift of Prayer

HELP KIDS LEARN WORDS OF PRAYER that will bring them comfort, strength, humility, trust, and faith in God!

Classic prayers are gifts that help us speak to God when we may not be able to come up with our own words. They also join us together when we gather in our homes and during worship. The easy-to-follow format of *Together We Pray* breaks prayers down into parts that are manageable for kids. Beautiful nature art adds to the joy of turning each page and taking steps in prayer.

You will be surprised how quickly and easily words of prayer take root in young hearts and minds. May the time and the prayers you share together be a blessing that you will cherish beyond these childhood years.

The Lord's Prayer

Our Father,

Who art in heaven,

hallowed be Thy name.

Thy kingdom come,
Thy will be done

on earth
as it is in heaven.

Give us this day

our daily bread,

and forgive us
our trespasses,

as we forgive those who trespass against us.

And lead us not into temptation,

but deliver us from evil.
Amen.

Hail Mary

Hail Mary, full of grace,

the Lord is with thee.

Blessed art thou

among women,

and blessed is the fruit

of thy womb, Jesus.

Holy Mary,

Mother of God,

pray for us sinners,

now and at the hour
of our death. Amen.

Glory Be

Glory be
to the Father,

and to the Son,

and to the Holy Spirit.

As it was
in the beginning,

is now,
and ever shall be,

world without end.
Amen.

Bless Us, O Lord

Bless us, O Lord,

and these Thy gifts,

which we are about
to receive

from Thy bounty,

through Christ
our Lord.

Amen.

Guardian Angel Prayer

Angel of God,

my guardian dear,

to whom God's love
commits me here,

ever this day,
be at my side,

to light and guard,

to rule and guide.
Amen.

Now I Lay Me Down to Sleep

Now I lay me

down to sleep,

I pray the Lord

my soul to keep.

May angels
watch me

through
the night,

and wake me with
the morning light.
Amen.

Prayer of Contrition

My God,
I am sorry

for my sins
with all my heart.

In choosing to do wrong

and failing to
do good,

I have sinned
against You

whom I should love
above all things.

I firmly intend,

with Your help,

to do penance,

to sin no more,

and to avoid whatever

leads me to sin.

Our Savior
Jesus Christ

suffered and
died for us.

In His name,
my God,

have mercy.
Amen.

Lamb of God

Lamb of God,
You take away

the sins of the world,

have mercy on us.

Lamb of God,
You take away

the sins of
the world,

have mercy on us.

Lamb of God,
You take away

the sins of
the world,

grant us peace.
Amen.

The Apostles' Creed

I believe in God,
the Father almighty,

Creator of
heaven and earth,

and in Jesus Christ,

His only Son, our Lord,

Who was conceived by the Holy Spirit,

born of
the Virgin Mary,

suffered under
Pontius Pilate,

was crucified, died,
and was buried.

He descended
into hell;

on the third day He rose again from the dead;

He ascended
into heaven,

and is seated at
the right hand
of God the Father
almighty;

from there
He shall come

to judge the living
and the dead.

I believe in the Holy Spirit,

the holy
catholic Church,

the communion
of saints,

the forgiveness
of sins,

the resurrection
of the body,

and life everlasting.
Amen.

Prayer of St. Patrick

(Adapted)

I arise today

through a mighty strength,

trusting in the power of Jesus Christ,

Son of the Living God.

Christ with me,
Christ before me,

Christ behind me,
Christ in me,

Christ beneath me,
Christ above me,

Christ on my right,
Christ on my left,

Christ when I lie down,

Christ when I sit down,

Christ in the heart of all
who think of me,

Christ in the mouth of all
who speak of me,

Christ in the eye
that sees me,

Christ in the ear
that hears me.

I arise today

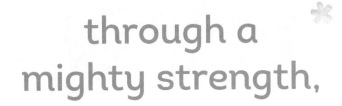

through a
mighty strength,

trusting in the power
of Jesus Christ,

Son of the Living God.
Amen.

Prayer of St. Francis of Assisi

Lord, make me
an instrument

of Your peace:

where there is hatred,
let me sow love;

where there is injury,
pardon;

where there is doubt,
faith;

where there is despair,
hope;

where there is darkness,
light;

where there is sadness,
joy.

O Divine Master,

grant that I may not
so much seek

to be consoled
as to console;

to be understood
as to understand;

to be loved
as to love.

For it is in giving
that we receive;

it is in pardoning
that we are pardoned;

and it is in dying

that we are born
to eternal life.
Amen.

Glory to God in the Highest

Glory to God

in the highest,

and peace to
his people on earth.

Lord God,
heavenly King,

almighty God
and Father,

we worship You,

we give You thanks,

we praise You
for Your glory.

Lord Jesus Christ,

only Son of the Father,

Lord God,

Lamb of God,

You take away
the sin of the world:

have mercy on us;

You are seated
at the right hand
of the Father:

receive our prayer.

For You alone
are the Holy One,

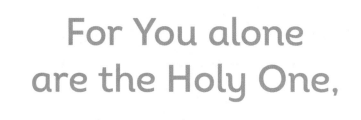

You alone are the Lord,

You alone are
the Most High,

Jesus Christ,

with the Holy Spirit,

in the glory of
God the Father.
Amen.

Hail, Holy Queen

Hail, holy Queen,

mother of Mercy.

Hail, our life,

our sweetness
and our hope.

To thee do we cry,

poor banished
children of Eve;

to thee do we

send up our sighs,

mourning
and weeping

in this vale
of tears.

Turn then,
most gracious
advocate,

thine eyes of mercy

toward us;

and after this our exile,
show unto us

the blessed fruit
of thy womb, Jesus.

O clement, O loving,
O sweet
virgin Mary.
Amen.

Prayer
to the
Holy Spirit

Come, Holy Spirit,

fill the hearts
of Your faithful,

and kindle in them

the fire of Your love.

Send forth
Your Spirit

and they shall
be created,

and You will renew

the face of the earth.
Amen.

Sign of the Cross

In the name
of the Father,
and of the Son,
and of the
Holy Spirit.
Amen.